DAILY KID QUOTES

Made in the USA
Las Vegas, NV
04 February 2022

43080798R00069